LYMPHEDEMA DIET

MEGA BUNDLE – 2 Manuscripts in 1 – 80+ Lymphedema - friendly recipes including breakfast, side dishes and dessert recipes

TABLE OF CONTENTS

BREAKFAST 7

PEAR PANCAKES 7

ALMOND PANCAKES 8

AVOCADO PANCAKES 9

STRAWBERRY PANCAKES 10

CARAMBOLA PANCAKES 11

GINGER MUFFINS 12

CARROT MUFFINS 14

BLUEBERRY MUFFINS 16

COCONUT MUFFINS 18

RAISIN MUFFINS 20

MUFFINS 22

PARMESAN OMELETTE 24

ASPARAGUS OMELETTE 25

ONION OMELETTE 26

OLIVE OMELETTE 27

TOMATO OMELETTE 28

BEANS OMELETTE 29

BREAKFAST GRANOLA 30

PEAR PANCAKES 31

ALMOND PANCAKES 32

AVOCADO PANCAKES 33

STRAWBERRY PANCAKES 34

CARAMBOLA PANCAKES 35

RAISIN BREAKFAST MIX 36

SAUSAGE BREAKFAST SANDWICH 37

STRAWBERRY MUFFINS	38
DESSERTS	40
BREAKFAST COOKIES	40
CHOCHOLATE TART	41
OREO PIE	42
GRAPEFRUIT PIE	43
BUTTERFINGER PIE	44
STRAWBERRY PIE	46
SMOOTHIES AND DRINKS	48
BANANA MATCHA SMOOTHIE	48
PROTEIN SMOOTHIE	49
CREAMY SMOOTHIE	50
POMEGRANATE SMOOTHIE	51
APPLE SMOOTHIE	52
SPINACH SMOOTHIE	53
PEANUT BUTTER SMOOTHIE	54
PINEAPPLE SMOOTHIE	55
ORANGE SMOOTHIE	56
RAISIN DATE SMOOTHIE	57
SECOND COOKBOOK	58
SOUP RECIPES	59
ONION SOUP	59
ZUCCHINI SOUP	61
SAUERKRAUT SOUP	63
GREEK RICE SOUP	65
GAZPACHO	67
TORTELLINI SOUP	68
LEBANESE SOUP	69

BROCCOLI SOUP	71
SWEET POTATO SOUP	72
SIDE DISHES	73
ZUCCHINI CHIPS	73
FRENCH POT ROAST	74
LEFTOVER TURKEY WITH SQUASH	75
PARMESAN DRUMSTICKS	76
SWEDISH MEATBALLS	77
ZUCCHINI LASAGNA	79
ACORN SQUASH WITH APPLES	81
CHICKEN LETTUCE WRAPS	82
CUP CHICKEN	83
SPAGHETTI WITH MEATBALLS	85
BASIL CHICKEN WITH BROCCOLI	86
CHEESE SAUCE	87
ZUCCHINI CHORIZO BUTTER	88
TARRAGON ZUCCHINI	89
GREEN PESTO PASTA	90
CRANBERRY SALAD	91
GAZPACHO SALAD	92
RADISH & PARSLEY SALAD	93
ZUCCHINI & BELL PEPPER SALAD	94
QUINOA & AVOCADO SALAD	95
TOFU SALAD	96
MIXED GREENS SALAD	97
QUINOA SALAD	98
ASPARAGUS FRITATTA	99
BEETS FRITATTA	100

ARTICHOKE FRITATTA	101
HAM FRITATTA	102
BROCCOLI FRITATTA	103
ROASTED SQUASH	104
PIZZA	**105**
ZUCCHINI PIZZA	105
SIMPLE PIZZA RECIPE	106
MUSHROOM PIZZA	107

Copyright 2020 by Noah Jerris - All rights reserved.

This document is geared towards providing exact and reliable information in regards to the topic and issue covered. The publication is sold with the idea that the publisher is not required to render accounting, officially permitted, or otherwise, qualified services. If advice is necessary, legal or professional, a practiced individual in the profession should be ordered.

- From a Declaration of Principles which was accepted and approved equally by a Committee of the American Bar Association and a Committee of Publishers and Associations.

In no way is it legal to reproduce, duplicate, or transmit any part of this document in either electronic means or in printed format. Recording of this publication is strictly prohibited and any storage of this document is not allowed unless with written permission from the publisher. All rights reserved.

The information provided herein is stated to be truthful and consistent, in that any liability, in terms of inattention or otherwise, by any usage or abuse of any policies, processes, or directions contained within is the solitary and utter responsibility of the recipient reader. Under no circumstances will any legal responsibility or blame be held against the publisher for any reparation, damages, or monetary loss due to the information herein, either directly or indirectly.

Respective authors own all copyrights not held by the publisher.

The information herein is offered for informational purposes solely, and is universal as so. The presentation of the information is without contract or any type of guarantee assurance.

The trademarks that are used are without any consent, and the publication of the trademark is without permission or backing by the trademark owner. All trademarks and brands within this book are for clarifying purposes only and are the owned by the owners themselves, not affiliated with this document.

Introduction

Lymphedema recipes for personal enjoyment but also for family enjoyment. You will love them for sure for how easy it is to prepare them.

BREAKFAST

PEAR PANCAKES

Serves: **4**
Prep Time: **10** Minutes

Cook Time: **20** Minutes

Total Time: **30** Minutes

INGREDIENTS

- 1 cup whole wheat flour
- ¼ tsp baking soda
- ¼ tsp baking powder
- 1 cup pears
- 2 eggs
- 1 cup milk

DIRECTIONS

1. In a bowl combine all ingredients together and mix well
2. In a skillet heat olive oil
3. Pour ¼ of the batter and cook each pancake for 1-2 minutes per side
4. When ready remove from heat and serve

ALMOND PANCAKES

Serves: **4**

Prep Time: **10** Minutes

Cook Time: **30** Minutes

Total Time: **40** Minutes

INGREDIENTS

- 1 cup whole wheat flour
- ¼ tsp baking soda
- ¼ tsp baking powder
- 1 cup almonds
- 2 eggs
- 1 cup milk

DIRECTIONS

1. **In a bowl combine all ingredients together and mix well**
2. **In a skillet heat olive oil**
3. **Pour ¼ of the batter and cook each pancake for 1-2 minutes per side**
4. **When ready remove from heat and serve**

AVOCADO PANCAKES

Serves: **4**

Prep Time: **10** Minutes

Cook Time: **20** Minutes

Total Time: **30** Minutes

INGREDIENTS

- 1 cup whole wheat flour
- ¼ tsp baking soda
- ¼ tsp baking powder
- 2 eggs
- 1 cup milk
- 1cup mashed avocado

DIRECTIONS

1. In a bowl combine all ingredients together and mix well
2. In a skillet heat olive oil
3. Pour ¼ of the batter and cook each pancake for 1-2 minutes per side
4. When ready remove from heat and serve

STRAWBERRY PANCAKES

Serves: **4**

Prep Time: **10** Minutes

Cook Time: **20** Minutes

Total Time: **30** Minutes

INGREDIENTS

- 1 cup whole wheat flour
- ¼ tsp baking soda
- ¼ tsp baking powder
- 1 cup strawberries
- 2 eggs
- 1 cup milk

DIRECTIONS

1. In a bowl combine all ingredients together and mix well
2. In a skillet heat olive oil
3. Pour ¼ of the batter and cook each pancake for 1-2 minutes per side
4. When ready remove from heat and serve

CARAMBOLA PANCAKES

Serves: **4**

Prep Time: **10** Minutes

Cook Time: **30** Minutes

Total Time: **40** Minutes

INGREDIENTS

- 1 cup whole wheat flour
- ¼ tsp baking soda
- ¼ tsp baking powder
- 2 eggs
- 1 cup milk
- 1 cup carambola

DIRECTIONS

1. In a bowl combine all ingredients together and mix well
2. In a skillet heat olive oil
3. Pour ¼ of the batter and cook each pancake for 1-2 minutes per side
4. When ready remove from heat and serve

GINGER MUFFINS

Serves: **8-12**
Prep Time: **10** Minutes
Cook Time: **20** Minutes
Total Time: **30** Minutes

INGREDIENTS

- 2 eggs
- 1 tablespoon olive oil
- 1 cup milk
- 2 cups whole wheat flour
- 1 tsp baking soda
- ¼ tsp baking soda
- 1 tsp ginger
- 1 tsp cinnamon
- ¼ cup molasses

DIRECTIONS

1. In a bowl combine all wet ingredients
2. In another bowl combine all dry ingredients
3. Combine wet and dry ingredients together
4. Fold in ginger and mix well

5. Pour mixture into 8-12 prepared muffin cups, fill 2/3 of the cups
6. Bake for 18-20 minutes at 375 F
7. When ready remove from the oven and serve

CARROT MUFFINS

Serves: **8-12**

Prep Time: **10** Minutes

Cook Time: **20** Minutes

Total Time: **30** Minutes

INGREDIENTS

- 2 eggs
- 1 tablespoon olive oil
- 1 cup milk
- 2 cups whole wheat flour
- 1 tsp baking soda
- ¼ tsp baking soda
- 1 tsp cinnamon
- 1 cup carrots

DIRECTIONS

1. In a bowl combine all wet ingredients
2. In another bowl combine all dry ingredients
3. Combine wet and dry ingredients together
4. Pour mixture into 8-12 prepared muffin cups, fill 2/3 of the cups

5. Bake for 18-20 minutes at 375 F
6. When ready remove from the oven and serve

BLUEBERRY MUFFINS

Serves: **8-12**

Prep Time: **10** Minutes

Cook Time: **20** Minutes

Total Time: **30** Minutes

INGREDIENTS

- 2 eggs
- 1 tablespoon olive oil
- 1 cup milk
- 2 cups whole wheat flour
- 1 tsp baking soda
- ¼ tsp baking soda
- 1 tsp cinnamon
- 1 cup blueberries

DIRECTIONS

1. In a bowl combine all wet ingredients
2. In another bowl combine all dry ingredients
3. Combine wet and dry ingredients together
4. Fold in blueberries and mix well

5. Pour mixture into 8-12 prepared muffin cups, fill 2/3 of the cups
6. Bake for 18-20 minutes at 375 F
7. When ready remove from the oven and serve

COCONUT MUFFINS

Serves: *8-12*

Prep Time: *10* Minutes

Cook Time: *20* Minutes

Total Time: *30* Minutes

INGREDIENTS

- 2 eggs
- 1 tablespoon olive oil
- 1 cup milk
- 2 cups whole wheat flour
- 1 tsp baking soda
- ¼ tsp baking soda
- 1 tsp cinnamon
- 1 cup coconut flakes

DIRECTIONS

1. In a bowl combine all wet ingredients
2. In another bowl combine all dry ingredients
3. Combine wet and dry ingredients together
4. Pour mixture into 8-12 prepared muffin cups, fill 2/3 of the cups

5. Bake for 18-20 minutes at 375 F
6. When ready remove from the oven and serve

RAISIN MUFFINS

Serves: **8-12**

Prep Time: **10** Minutes

Cook Time: **20** Minutes

Total Time: **30** Minutes

INGREDIENTS

- 2 eggs
- 1 tablespoon olive oil
- 1 cup milk
- 2 cups whole wheat flour
- 1 tsp baking soda
- ¼ tsp baking soda
- 1 tsp cinnamon
- 1 cup raisins

DIRECTIONS

1. In a bowl combine all wet ingredients
2. In another bowl combine all dry ingredients
3. Combine wet and dry ingredients together
4. Pour mixture into 8-12 prepared muffin cups, fill 2/3 of the cups

5. Bake for 18-20 minutes at 375 F
6. When ready remove from the oven and serve

MUFFINS

Serves: *8-12*

Prep Time: *10* Minutes

Cook Time: *20* Minutes

Total Time: *30* Minutes

INGREDIENTS

- 2 eggs
- 1 tablespoon olive oil
- 1 cup milk
- 2 cups whole wheat flour
- 1 tsp baking soda
- ¼ tsp baking soda
- 1 tsp cinnamon

DIRECTIONS

1. In a bowl combine all wet ingredients
2. In another bowl combine all dry ingredients
3. Combine wet and dry ingredients together
4. Pour mixture into 8-12 prepared muffin cups, fill 2/3 of the cups
5. Bake for 18-20 minutes at 375 F

6. When ready remove from the oven and serve

PARMESAN OMELETTE

Serves: **1**

Prep Time: **5** Minutes

Cook Time: **10** Minutes

Total Time: **15** Minutes

INGREDIENTS

- 2 eggs
- ¼ tsp salt
- ¼ tsp black pepper
- 1 tablespoon olive oil
- ¼ cup parmesan cheese
- ¼ tsp basil

DIRECTIONS

1. In a bowl combine all ingredients together and mix well
2. In a skillet heat olive oil and pour the egg mixture
3. Cook for 1-2 minutes per side
4. When ready remove omelette from the skillet and serve

ASPARAGUS OMELETTE

Serves: *1*
Prep Time: *5*   Minutes
Cook Time: *10* Minutes
Total Time: *15* Minutes

INGREDIENTS

- 2 eggs
- ¼ tsp salt
- ¼ tsp black pepper
- 1 tablespoon olive oil
- ¼ cup cheese
- ¼ tsp basil
- 1 cup asparagus

DIRECTIONS

1. In a bowl combine all ingredients together and mix well
2. In a skillet heat olive oil and pour the egg mixture
3. Cook for 1-2 minutes per side
4. When ready remove omelette from the skillet and serve

ONION OMELETTE

Serves: *1*

Prep Time: *5* Minutes

Cook Time: *10* Minutes

Total Time: *15* Minutes

INGREDIENTS

- 2 eggs
- ¼ tsp salt
- ¼ tsp black pepper
- 1 tablespoon olive oil
- ¼ cup cheese
- ¼ tsp basil
- 1 cup red onion

DIRECTIONS

1. In a bowl combine all ingredients together and mix well
2. In a skillet heat olive oil and pour the egg mixture
3. Cook for 1-2 minutes per side
4. When ready remove omelette from the skillet and serve

OLIVE OMELETTE

Serves: *1*
Prep Time: **5** Minutes
Cook Time: **10** Minutes
Total Time: **15** Minutes

INGREDIENTS

- 2 eggs
- ¼ tsp salt
- ¼ tsp black pepper
- 1 tablespoon olive oil
- ¼ cup cheese
- ¼ tsp basil
- ½ cup olives

DIRECTIONS

1. In a bowl combine all ingredients together and mix well
2. In a skillet heat olive oil and pour the egg mixture
3. Cook for 1-2 minutes per side
4. When ready remove omelette from the skillet and serve

TOMATO OMELETTE

Serves: **1**
Prep Time: **5** Minutes
Cook Time: **10** Minutes
Total Time: **15** Minutes

INGREDIENTS

- 2 eggs
- ¼ tsp salt
- ¼ tsp black pepper
- 1 tablespoon olive oil
- ¼ cup cheese
- ¼ tsp basil
- 1 cup tomatoes

DIRECTIONS

1. In a bowl combine all ingredients together and mix well
2. In a skillet heat olive oil and pour the egg mixture
3. Cook for 1-2 minutes per side
4. When ready remove omelette from the skillet and serve

BEANS OMELETTE

Serves: *1*
Prep Time: *5* Minutes
Cook Time: *10* Minutes
Total Time: *15* Minutes

INGREDIENTS

- 2 eggs
- ¼ tsp salt
- ¼ tsp black pepper
- 1 tablespoon olive oil
- ¼ cup cheese
- ¼ tsp basil
- 1 cup beans

DIRECTIONS

1. In a bowl combine all ingredients together and mix well
2. In a skillet heat olive oil and pour the egg mixture
3. Cook for 1-2 minutes per side
4. When ready remove omelette from the skillet and serve

BREAKFAST GRANOLA

Serves: 2
Prep Time: 5   Minutes
Cook Time: 30 Minutes
Total Time: 35 Minutes

INGREDIENTS

- 1 tsp vanilla extract
- 1 tablespoon honey
- 1 lb. rolled oats
- 2 tablespoons sesame seeds
- ¼ lb. almonds
- ¼ lb. berries

DIRECTIONS

1. **Preheat the oven to 325 F**
2. **Spread the granola onto a baking sheet**
3. **Bake for 12-15 minutes, remove and mix everything**
4. **Bake for another 12-15 minutes or until slightly brown**
5. **When ready remove from the oven and serve**

PEAR PANCAKES

Serves: **4**

Prep Time: **10** Minutes

Cook Time: **20** Minutes

Total Time: **30** Minutes

INGREDIENTS

- 1 cup whole wheat flour
- ¼ tsp baking soda
- ¼ tsp baking powder
- 1 cup pears
- 2 eggs
- 1 cup milk

DIRECTIONS

1. In a bowl combine all ingredients together and mix well
2. In a skillet heat olive oil
3. Pour ¼ of the batter and cook each pancake for 1-2 minutes per side
4. When ready remove from heat and serve

ALMOND PANCAKES

Serves: **4**

Prep Time: **10** Minutes

Cook Time: **30** Minutes

Total Time: **40** Minutes

INGREDIENTS

- 1 cup whole wheat flour
- ¼ tsp baking soda
- ¼ tsp baking powder
- 1 cup almonds
- 2 eggs
- 1 cup milk

DIRECTIONS

1. **In a bowl combine all ingredients together and mix well**
2. **In a skillet heat olive oil**
3. **Pour ¼ of the batter and cook each pancake for 1-2 minutes per side**
4. **When ready remove from heat and serve**

AVOCADO PANCAKES

Serves: **4**

Prep Time: **10** Minutes

Cook Time: **20** Minutes

Total Time: **30** Minutes

INGREDIENTS

- 1 cup whole wheat flour
- ¼ tsp baking soda
- ¼ tsp baking powder
- 2 eggs
- 1 cup milk
- 1cup mashed avocado

DIRECTIONS

1. In a bowl combine all ingredients together and mix well
2. In a skillet heat olive oil
3. Pour ¼ of the batter and cook each pancake for 1-2 minutes per side
4. When ready remove from heat and serve

STRAWBERRY PANCAKES

Serves: **4**

Prep Time: **10** Minutes

Cook Time: **20** Minutes

Total Time: **30** Minutes

INGREDIENTS

- 1 cup whole wheat flour
- ¼ tsp baking soda
- ¼ tsp baking powder
- 1 cup strawberries
- 2 eggs
- 1 cup milk

DIRECTIONS

1. In a bowl combine all ingredients together and mix well
2. In a skillet heat olive oil
3. Pour ¼ of the batter and cook each pancake for 1-2 minutes per side
4. When ready remove from heat and serve

CARAMBOLA PANCAKES

Serves: **4**
Prep Time: **10** Minutes

Cook Time: **30** Minutes

Total Time: **40** Minutes

INGREDIENTS

- 1 cup whole wheat flour
- ¼ tsp baking soda
- ¼ tsp baking powder
- 2 eggs
- 1 cup milk
- 1 cup carambola

DIRECTIONS

1. In a bowl combine all ingredients together and mix well
2. In a skillet heat olive oil
3. Pour ¼ of the batter and cook each pancake for 1-2 minutes per side
4. When ready remove from heat and serve

RAISIN BREAKFAST MIX

Serves: **1**

Prep Time: **5** Minutes

Cook Time: **5** Minutes

Total Time: **10** Minutes

INGREDIENTS

- ½ cup dried raisins
- ½ cup dried pecans
- ¼ cup almonds
- 1 cup coconut milk
- 1 tsp cinnamon

DIRECTIONS

1. **In a bowl combine all ingredients together**
2. **Serve with milk**

SAUSAGE BREAKFAST SANDWICH

Serves: 2

Prep Time: 5 Minutes

Cook Time: 15 Minutes

Total Time: 20 Minutes

INGREDIENTS

- ¼ cup egg substitute
- 1 muffin
- 1 turkey sausage patty
- 1 tablespoon cheddar cheese

DIRECTIONS

1. In a skillet pour egg and cook on low heat
2. Place turkey sausage patty in a pan and cook for 4-5 minutes per side
3. On a toasted muffin place the cooked egg, top with a sausage patty and cheddar cheese
4. Serve when ready

STRAWBERRY MUFFINS

Serves: **8-12**

Prep Time: **10** Minutes

Cook Time: **20** Minutes

Total Time: **30** Minutes

INGREDIENTS

- 2 eggs
- 1 tablespoon olive oil
- 1 cup milk
- 2 cups whole wheat flour
- 1 tsp baking soda
- ¼ tsp baking soda
- 1 tsp cinnamon
- 1 cup strawberries

DIRECTIONS

1. In a bowl combine all wet ingredients
2. In another bowl combine all dry ingredients
3. Combine wet and dry ingredients together
4. Pour mixture into 8-12 prepared muffin cups, fill 2/3 of the cups

5. Bake for 18-20 minutes at 375 F
6. When ready remove from the oven and serve

DESSERTS

BREAKFAST COOKIES

Serves: *8-12*

Prep Time: *5* Minutes

Cook Time: *15* Minutes

Total Time: *20* Minutes

INGREDIENTS

- 1 cup rolled oats
- ¼ cup applesauce
- ½ tsp vanilla extract
- 3 tablespoons chocolate chips
- 2 tablespoons dried fruits
- 1 tsp cinnamon

DIRECTIONS

1. Preheat the oven to 325 F
2. In a bowl combine all ingredients together and mix well
3. Scoop cookies using an ice cream scoop
4. Place cookies onto a prepared baking sheet
5. Place in the oven for 12-15 minutes or until the cookies are done
6. When ready remove from the oven and serve

CHOCHOLATE TART

Serves: **6-8**
Prep Time: **25** Minutes
Cook Time: **25** Minutes
Total Time: **50** Minutes

INGREDIENTS

- pastry sheets
- 1 tsp vanilla extract
- ½ lb. caramel
- ½ lb. black chocolate
- 4-5 tablespoons butter
- 3 eggs
- ¼ lb. brown sugar

DIRECTIONS

1. Preheat oven to 400 F, unfold pastry sheets and place them on a baking sheet
2. Toss together all ingredients together and mix well
3. Spread mixture in a single layer on the pastry sheets
4. Before baking decorate with your desired fruits
5. Bake at 400 F for 22-25 minutes or until golden brown

OREO PIE

Serves: **8-12**

Prep Time: **15** Minutes

Cook Time: **35** Minutes

Total Time: **50** Minutes

INGREDIENTS

- pastry sheets
- 6-8 oz. chocolate crumb piecrust
- 1 cup half-and-half
- 1 package instant pudding mix
- 10-12 Oreo cookies
- 10 oz. whipped topping

DIRECTIONS

1. Line a pie plate or pie form with pastry and cover the edges of the plate depending on your preference
2. In a bowl combine all pie ingredients together and mix well
3. Pour the mixture over the pastry
4. Bake at 400-425 F for 25-30 minutes or until golden brown
5. When ready remove from the oven and let it rest for 15 minutes

GRAPEFRUIT PIE

Serves: *8-12*

Prep Time: *15* Minutes

Cook Time: *35* Minutes

Total Time: *50* Minutes

INGREDIENTS

- pastry sheets
- 2 cups grapefruit
- 1 cup brown sugar
- ¼ cup flour
- 5-6 egg yolks
- 5 oz. butter

DIRECTIONS

1. Line a pie plate or pie form with pastry and cover the edges of the plate depending on your preference
2. In a bowl combine all pie ingredients together and mix well
3. Pour the mixture over the pastry
4. Bake at 400-425 F for 25-30 minutes or until golden brown
5. When ready remove from the oven and let it rest for 15 minutes

BUTTERFINGER PIE

Serves: *8-12*

Prep Time: *15* Minutes

Cook Time: *35* Minutes

Total Time: *50* Minutes

INGREDIENTS

- pastry sheets
- 1 package cream cheese
- 1 tsp vanilla extract
- ¼ cup peanut butter
- 1 cup powdered sugar (to decorate)
- 2 cups Butterfinger candy bars
- 8 oz whipped topping

DIRECTIONS

1. Line a pie plate or pie form with pastry and cover the edges of the plate depending on your preference
2. In a bowl combine all pie ingredients together and mix well
3. Pour the mixture over the pastry
4. Bake at 400-425 F for 25-30 minutes or until golden brown

5. When ready remove from the oven and let it rest for 15 minutes

STRAWBERRY PIE

Serves: **8-12**

Prep Time: **15** Minutes

Cook Time: **35** Minutes

Total Time: **50** Minutes

INGREDIENTS

- pastry sheets
- 1,5 lb. strawberries
- 1 cup powdered sugar
- 2 tablespoons cornstarch
- 1 tablespoon lime juice
- 1 tsp vanilla extract
- 2 eggs
- 2 tablespoons butter

DIRECTIONS

1. Line a pie plate or pie form with pastry and cover the edges of the plate depending on your preference
2. In a bowl combine all pie ingredients together and mix well
3. Pour the mixture over the pastry
4. Bake at 400-425 F for 25-30 minutes or until golden brown

5. When ready remove from the oven and let it rest for 15 minutes

SMOOTHIES AND DRINKS

BANANA MATCHA SMOOTHIE

Serves: *1*

Prep Time: *5* Minutes

Cook Time: *5* Minutes

Total Time: *10* Minutes

INGREDIENTS

- 1 cup banana
- 1 tsp matcha powder
- 1 cup spinach
- 1 tsp flax seed
- 1 tsp vanilla extract
- 1 cup soy milk

DIRECTIONS

1. In a blender place all ingredients and blend until smooth
2. Pour smoothie in a glass and serve

PROTEIN SMOOTHIE

Serves: *1*

Prep Time: *5* Minutes

Cook Time: *5* Minutes

Total Time: *10* Minutes

INGREDIENTS

- 2 bananas
- 2 dates
- 1 cup kale
- 1 cup spinach
- 2 tablespoons cocoa powder
- 1 tsp vanilla extract
- 1 cup nut milk

DIRECTIONS

1. **In a blender place all ingredients and blend until smooth**
2. **Pour smoothie in a glass and serve**

CREAMY SMOOTHIE

Serves: **1**

Prep Time: **5** Minutes

Cook Time: **5** Minutes

Total Time: **10** Minutes

INGREDIENTS

- 1 cup strawberries
- 1 banana
- 1 cup Greek Yogurt
- 1 cup soy milk
- 1 tsp vanilla extract
- 1 tsp chia seeds

DIRECTIONS

1. **In a blender place all ingredients and blend until smooth**
2. **Pour smoothie in a glass and serve**

POMEGRANATE SMOOTHIE

Serves: *1*
Prep Time: *5* Minutes
Cook Time: *5* Minutes
Total Time: *10* Minutes

INGREDIENTS

- 1 cup strawberries
- 1 banana
- 1 cup Greek Yogurt
- 1 scoop protein powder
- 1 tsp hemp seeds
- ½ cup chocolate chips

DIRECTIONS

1. In a blender place all ingredients and blend until smooth
2. Pour smoothie in a glass and serve

APPLE SMOOTHIE

Serves: *1*

Prep Time: *5* Minutes

Cook Time: *5* Minutes

Total Time: *10* Minutes

INGREDIENTS

- 1 apple
- 2 pears
- ½ cup rolled oats
- 1 tsp cinnamon
- 1 cup nut milk

DIRECTIONS

1. In a blender place all ingredients and blend until smooth
2. Pour smoothie in a glass and serve

SPINACH SMOOTHIE

Serves: *1*

Prep Time: *5* Minutes

Cook Time: *5* Minutes

Total Time: *10* Minutes

INGREDIENTS

- 1 banana
- 1 cup vanilla yogurt
- 1 cup spinach
- 1 cup kale
- 1 cup orange juice

DIRECTIONS

1. **In a blender place all ingredients and blend until smooth**
2. **Pour smoothie in a glass and serve**

PEANUT BUTTER SMOOTHIE

Serves: *1*

Prep Time: *5* Minutes

Cook Time: *5* Minutes

Total Time: *10* Minutes

INGREDIENTS

- 1 cup berries
- 2 tablespoons peanut butter
- ½ cup protein powder
- ½ cup oats
- 1 cup soy milk

DIRECTIONS

1. **In a blender place all ingredients and blend until smooth**
2. **Pour smoothie in a glass and serve**

PINEAPPLE SMOOTHIE

Serves: *1*

Prep Time: *5* Minutes

Cook Time: *5* Minutes

Total Time: *10* Minutes

INGREDIENTS

- 1 cup pineapple
- 1 cup strawberries
- 1 cup Greek yogurt
- 1 cup soy milk
- 1 cup ice

DIRECTIONS

1. In a blender place all ingredients and blend until smooth
2. Pour smoothie in a glass and serve

ORANGE SMOOTHIE

Serves: **1**

Prep Time: **5** Minutes

Cook Time: **5** Minutes

Total Time: **10** Minutes

INGREDIENTS

- 1 orange
- ½ cup orange juice
- ½ banana
- 1 tsp vanilla essence

DIRECTIONS

1. **In a blender place all ingredients and blend until smooth**
2. **Pour smoothie in a glass and serve**

RAISIN DATE SMOOTHIE

Serves: *1*

Prep Time: *5* Minutes

Cook Time: *5* Minutes

Total Time: *10* Minutes

INGREDIENTS

- ¼ cup raisins
- 2 Medjool dates
- 1 cup berries
- 1 cup almond milk
- 1 tsp chia seeds

DIRECTIONS

1. In a blender place all ingredients and blend until smooth
2. Pour smoothie in a glass and serve

SECOND COOKBOOK

SOUP RECIPES

ONION SOUP

Serves: **4**

Prep Time: **10** Minutes

Cook Time: **20** Minutes

Total Time: **30** Minutes

INGREDIENTS

- 6 spring onions
- ½ red onion
- 1 potato
- 1 tablespoon olive oil
- Salt
- ¼ tsp coriander

DIRECTIONS

1. **In a pot place the potatoes, water and boil until the potatoes are soft**
2. **In another pot heat olive oil and sauté spring onions and onion until soft**
3. **Add boiled potatoes to the pot where are the sauté onions**
4. **Add coriander, salt, pepper and stir well**
5. **Blend the soup until the soup is creamy**

6. When ready pour into bowls and serve

ZUCCHINI SOUP

Serves: **6**

Prep Time: **10** Minutes

Cook Time: **25** Minutes

Total Time: **35** Minutes

INGREDIENTS

- 1 onion
- 1 tsp olive oil
- 1 zucchini
- 1 cup corn
- 1 cup broth
- 1 cup soy yogurt
- 1 tsp red pepper flakes
- 1 tablespoon cilantro
- 1 tablespoon parmesan

DIRECTIONS

1. In a skillet sauté onion until soft
2. Add zucchinis, corn and sauté for 5-6 minutes
3. Stir in water, vegetable broth, black pepper and salt
4. Bring everything to a boil and cook for 8-10 minutes
5. Add soy yogurt, cilantro, red pepper flakes and cook for another 5-6 minutes

6. When ready ad parmesan and serve

SAUERKRAUT SOUP

Serves: **4**

Prep Time: **10** Minutes

Cook Time: **30** Minutes

Total Time: **40** Minutes

INGREDIENTS

- 2 celery sticks
- 1 onion
- 2 carrots
- 2 potatoes
- 1 cup mushrooms
- 1 cup sauerkraut
- 6 cups vegetable broth
- 1 tablespoon olive oil
- 1 cup tofu
- 1 bay leaf

DIRECTIONS

1. In a pot heat olive oil and add tofu
2. Cook until crispy and set aside
3. Sauté onion and mushrooms for 2-3 minutes
4. Add vegetable broth and the rest of the ingredients

5. Bring everything to a boil and simmer on low heat for 18-20 minutes
6. When the soup is ready remove the bay leaf and transfer soup to a blender
7. Blend until smooth and serve with tofu slices on top

GREEK RICE SOUP

Serves: **6**

Prep Time: **10** Minutes

Cook Time: **35** Minutes

Total Time: **45** Minutes

INGREDIENTS

- 1 onion
- 1 carrot
- 1 cup celery
- 4 cups vegetable broth
- ¼ cup rice
- ½ cup tofu
- 1 tablespoon dill
- 1 lemon

EGG MIXTURE

- 1 cup coconut milk
- 1 cup tofu
- 2 tablespoons lemon juice
- 1 tsp salt
- 1 tsp black pepper
- 1 tsp nutritional yeast

DIRECTIONS

1. In a pot heat olive oil and add carrots, celery, onion and sauté until vegetables are soft
2. Add rice, vegetable broth and cook until the rice absorbs the liquid
3. In a blender add the ingredients for the egg mixture and blend until smooth
4. Pour the egg mixture into the soup and stir well
5. Add tofu, dill and any remaining ingredients to the soup
6. Cover and cook until the soup is ready

GAZPACHO

Serves: **2**

Prep Time: **10** Minutes

Cook Time: **10** Minutes

Total Time: **20** Minutes

INGREDIENTS

- 1 cucumber
- ½ cup tomato juice
- 4 tomatoes
- ¼ avocado
- 1 garlic clove
- ¼ red onion
- 2 tablespoons red wine vinegar
- 1 tablespoon olive oil
- black pepper

DIRECTIONS

1. In a blender add all ingredients for the soup and blend until smooth
2. Pour soup in a container add seasoning and mix well
3. Serve when ready and refrigerate remaining soup

TORTELLINI SOUP

Serves: **6**

Prep Time: **10** Minutes

Cook Time: **20** Minutes

Total Time: **30** Minutes

INGREDIENTS

- 1 cup crushed tomatoes
- 3 cups vegetable broth
- 1 tsp tomato paste
- 1 tsp basil
- 1 tsp oregano
- 2 cups mushrooms tortellini
- 2 cups baby spinach

DIRECTIONS

1. In a pot sauté onion and garlic
2. Ad tofu and cook until soft
3. Add the rest of the ingredients to the pot and cook for another 10-12 minutes
4. Cook until tortellini are done
5. When ready remove soup from heat and serve

LEBANESE SOUP

Serves: **4**

Prep Time: **10** Minutes

Cook Time: **25** Minutes

Total Time: **35** Minutes

INGREDIENTS

- 1 tablespoon olive oil
- 1 onion
- 1 carrot
- 1 large potato
- 1 garlic clove
- 1 bay leaf
- 1 cup cooked chickpeas
- 1 tomato
- 2 cups vegetable broth
- 1 cup water
- 1 tablespoon tomato pate
- 1 tsp paprika
- 1 tablespoon parsley

DIRECTIONS

1. In a saucepan sauté garlic and onion

2. Add tomatoes, carrots, potatoes and cook for another 4-5 minutes
3. Add remaining ingredients and bring soup to a boil
4. Simmer on low heat for 15-18 minutes
5. When ready remove from heat and serve

BROCCOLI SOUP

Serves: **4**

Prep Time: **10** Minutes

Cook Time: **15** Minutes

Total Time: **25** Minutes

INGREDIENTS

- 2 lb. broccoli
- 2 potatoes
- 2 garlic cloves
- 1 onion
- 2 tablespoons nutritional yeast
- 1 tablespoon olive oil
- 1 tsp salt

DIRECTIONS

1. In a pot add potatoes, broccoli, onion and sauté until vegetables are soft
2. Place saluted veggies in a blender, add garlic, nutritional yeast, salt and blend until smooth
3. Add remaining ingredients and blend again
4. When ready transfer to a plate, drizzle olive oil and serve

SWEET POTATO SOUP

Serves: **4**

Prep Time: **10** Minutes

Cook Time: **30** Minutes

Total Time: **40** Minutes

INGREDIENTS

- 3 sweet potatoes
- 1 onion
- 2 carrots
- ¼ tsp cumin
- ¼ tsp red pepper
- olive oil
- 1-inch piece ginger
- water

DIRECTIONS

1. Place all vegetables in a pot
2. Add water and bring to a boil
3. Boil on low heat for 25-30 minutes
4. When vegetables are tender blend soup
5. Add remaining ingredients and blend again
6. Pour soup into a bowl, season and serve

SIDE DISHES

ZUCCHINI CHIPS

Serves: **4**

Prep Time: **5** Minutes

Cook Time: **10** Hours

Total Time: **10** Hours 5 Minutes

INGREDIENTS

- 1 lb. zucchini
- 1 tablespoon oil
- 1 tsp salt

DIRECTIONS

1. Slice zucchini into thin slices
2. Toss in salt and oil
3. Arrange in a single on a dehydrator tray
4. Dehydrate at 125 F for 10-12 hours
5. When ready remove and serve

FRENCH POT ROAST

Serves: **4**

Prep Time: **10** Minutes

Cook Time: **7** Hours

Total Time: **7** Hours and 10 Minutes

INGREDIENTS

- 1 tablespoon butter
- 2 lbs. beef roast
- 1 onion
- 6 cloves garlic
- 3 slices bacon
- ¼ cup red wine
- ½ tsp rosemary
- ¼ tsp dried thyme
- pinch of salt

DIRECTIONS

1. In a skillet heat butter, add beef roast and brown on all sides, remove and place to a crock pot
2. Sauté onions, bacon, garlic and move to crock pot
3. Add onion, seasoning and cook on low for 6-7 hours

LEFTOVER TURKEY WITH SQUASH

Serves: 2
Prep Time: 10 Minutes
Cook Time: 50 Minutes
Total Time: 60 Minutes

INGREDIENTS

- 1 squash
- 1 onion
- 2 cup leftover turkey
- 2 apples
- 1 cup cranberries
- 1 tsp cinnamon
- 1 tsp salt
- ¼ tsp nutmeg
- ¼ cup butter

DIRECTIONS

1. Preheat oven to 325 F
2. Cut squash in half and slice into half rings and place in a bowl
3. Toss with spices, cranberries, apples
4. Pour into baking dish and bake for 40-50 minutes or until tender
5. Remove and serve

PARMESAN DRUMSTICKS

Serves: **3**

Prep Time: **10** Minutes

Cook Time: **40** Minutes

Total Time: **50** Minutes

INGREDIENTS

- 2 eggs
- 2 cups parmesan cheese
- 1 tsp salt
- 1 tsp black pepper
- 12 chicken drumsticks
- coconut oil

DIRECTIONS

1. **Preheat oven to 375 F**
2. **In a bowl crack eggs, beat them and set aside**
3. **In another bowl mix cheese, pepper, salt and set aside**
4. **Dip the drumsticks into the egg mixture and coat evenly**
5. **Roll into cheese mixture and place in the baking pan**
6. **Bake for 40-50 minutes, remove and serve**

SWEDISH MEATBALLS

Serves: **6**
Prep Time: **10** Minutes
Cook Time: **20** Minutes
Total Time: **30** Minutes

INGREDIENTS

- 1 cup sunflower oil
- ¼ cup coconut milk
- 1 tsp onion powder
- 1 tsp
- salt
- 4 lbs. ground beef
-
- 2 eggs
- 1 tsp black pepper
- ¼ tsp allspice
- ¼ tsp nutmeg

SAUCE

- ½ cup butter
- ¼ cup parmesan cheese
- 5 cups beef broth
- ¼ cup coconut milk
- salt

DIRECTIONS

1. Preheat oven to 375 F
2. In a bowl mix all meatballs ingredients using a stand mixer
3. Form little balls and bake for 20-25 minutes or until done
4. In a skillet sauce parmesan cheese, whisk in beef broth, salt, and coconut milk, cook until thickened
5. Serve on top of meatballs

ZUCCHINI LASAGNA

Serves: **6**

Prep Time: **10** Minutes

Cook Time: **20** Minutes

Total Time: **30** Minutes

INGREDIENTS

- 1 onion
- 3 cloves garlic
- 2 tablespoon butter
- 1 lb. ground beef
- 1 lb. Italian sausage
- 1 tablespoon oregano
- ¼ cup basil
- ¼ tsp cayenne pepper
- salt
- 14 oz. can diced tomatoes
- 6 oz. can tomato paste
- 4 zucchinis
- 3 cup cheddar cheese

DIRECTIONS

1. Preheat oven to 325 F
2. Slice the zucchinis into long strips
3. In a pot sauté the onions and garlic
4. Add Italian sausage, beef, basil, cayenne, pepper, oregano and cook for 5-6 minutes
5. Add tomato paste and tomatoes and cook for another 4-5 minutes
6. Bake for 40-45 minutes, remove and serve

ACORN SQUASH WITH APPLES

Serves: **4**

Prep Time: **10** Minutes

Cook Time: **30** Minutes

Total Time: **40** Minutes

INGREDIENTS

- 2 acorn squash
- ¼ cup butter
- ½ cup shallots
- 2 apples
- ¼ tsp salt
- ½ tsp black pepper
- ¼ tsp cinnamon
- ½ tsp nutmeg

DIRECTIONS

1. Preheat oven to 325 F
2. Bake squash for 20-25 minutes
3. Sauté the shallots until tender, add salt, pepper, apples, nutmeg, and cinnamon
4. Fill each squash with apple mixture, bake for 25-30 minutes
5. Remove and serve

CHICKEN LETTUCE WRAPS

Serves: **2**

Prep Time: **10** Minutes

Cook Time: **20** Minutes

Total Time: **30** Minutes

INGREDIENTS

- 2 lbs. ground chicken
- 2 onions
- 3 garlic cloves
- 1 yellow squash
- 1 bell pepper
- 1 bunch basil
- salt
- 1 cup Italian dressing
- 1 head romaine lettuce

DIRECTIONS

1. Cook ground chicken until tender with garlic, pepper, basil, onions, and squash
2. Serve the squash with lettuce leaves and Italian dressing

CUP CHICKEN

Serves: 2
Prep Time: 10 Minutes
Cook Time: 20 Minutes
Total Time: 30 Minutes

INGREDIENTS

- 2 tablespoons sesame oil
- 2-inch piece ginger
- 16-18 garlic cloves
- 1 tsp black pepper
- 1 pinch cloves
- 1,5 lbs. chicken drumsticks
- 2 tablespoons coconut aminos
- 1 tablespoon fish sauce
- 1 tablespoon honey
- 1 cup basil leaves

DIRECTIONS

1. In a skillet add sesame oil, pepper, cloves, garlic, ginger and sauté for 3-4 minutes
2. Add chicken and cook for 6-7 minutes, add honey coconut aminos, fish sauce and bring to boil
3. Lower the heat and simmer for 14-16 minutes

4. Add basil, stir to combine and serve when ready

SPAGHETTI WITH MEATBALLS

Serves: **12**

Prep Time: **10** Minutes

Cook Time: **20** Minutes

Total Time: **30** Minutes

INGREDIENTS

- 3 zucchinis
- 2 cups sauce
- 1 b. ground beef
- 1 onion
- 2 cloves garlic
- 1 tablespoon herbs
- 1 tablespoon butter

DIRECTIONS

1. Cook spaghetti squash and set aside
2. In a bowl mix garlic, seasoning, onion, ground beef, and divide into 12-14 meatballs
3. Add the meatballs into a pot and cook until they are browned
4. Add sauce, seasoning and simmer for 10-12 minutes
5. Add vegetable noodles cook until done and remove from heat
6. Add salt and serve

BASIL CHICKEN WITH BROCCOLI

Serves: **6**

Prep Time: **10** Minutes

Cook Time: **50** Minutes

Total Time: **60** Minutes

INGREDIENTS

- 2 lbs. chicken pieces drumsticks
- ½ cup parmesan cheese
- 2 tablespoons almond flour
- 1 tsp garlic powder
- 1 tsp dried basil 1 tsp salt
- black pepper
- 2 heads broccoli

DIRECTIONS

1. Preheat oven to 350 F
2. Lay chicken in a pan and sprinkle with garlic powder, parmesan basil, pepper and salt
3. Add 2 tablespoons butter and bake for 40-45 minutes
4. Remove from oven and transfer to a plate
5. Serve with baked broccoli

CHEESE SAUCE

Serves: 2
Prep Time: 5 Minutes
Cook Time: 5 Minutes
Total Time: 10 Minutes

INGREDIENTS

- 1 cup c
- oconut milk
- ½ cup gelatin (SCD Safe)
- 6 oz. cheddar cheese
- ¼ tsp salt

DIRECTIONS

1. In a saucepan heat milk and stir occasionally
2. Chop cheese into small chunks and place cheese in a blender
3. Add the milk and blend for 20-30 seconds
4. Pour into saucepan and lower heat
5. When ready remove and serve

ZUCCHINI CHORIZO BUTTER

Serves: *4*

Prep Time: *10* Minutes

Cook Time: *70* Minutes

Total Time: *80* Minutes

INGREDIENTS

- 2 lbs. zucchini
- 3 cups bone broth
- 1 cup chorizo
- 2 bell peppers
- 5 tablespoons butter

DIRECTIONS

1. Cut zucchini into ½ inch slices and place in a saucepan
2. Add bone broth and simmer for 25-30 minutes
3. Add peppers, chorizo and simmer for another 20 minutes
4. Stir in stew, butter and cook for another 10-12 minutes
5. Remove from heat and serve when ready

TARRAGON ZUCCHINI

Serves: **4**

Prep Time: **5** Minutes

Cook Time: **15** Minutes

Total Time: **20** Minutes

INGREDIENTS

- ¼ tablespoon butter
- 1 zucchini
- 1 tablespoon tarragon leaves
- ½ cup heavy cream

DIRECTIONS

1. In a pan melt butter over medium heat
2. Sauté the zucchini for 6-7 minutes, add tarragon and cook until tender
3. Remove and serve

GREEN PESTO PASTA

Serves: 2

Prep Time: 5 Minutes

Cook Time: 15 Minutes

Total Time: 20 Minutes

INGREDIENTS

- 4 oz. spaghetti
- 2 cups basil leaves
- 2 garlic cloves
- ¼ cup olive oil
- 2 tablespoons parmesan cheese
- ½ tsp black pepper

DIRECTIONS

6. Bring water to a boil and add pasta
7. In a blend add parmesan cheese, basil leaves, garlic and blend
8. Add olive oil, pepper and blend again
9. Pour pesto onto pasta and serve when ready

CRANBERRY SALAD

Serves: 2
Prep Time: 5 Minutes
Cook Time: 15 Minutes
Total Time: 20 Minutes

INGREDIENTS

- ½ cup celery
- 1 packet Knox Gelatin
- 1 cup cranberry juice
- 1 can berry cranberry sauce
- 1 cup sour cream

DIRECTIONS

1. In a pan add juice, gelatin, cranberry sauce and cook on low heat
2. Add sour cream, celery and continue to cook
3. Pour mixture into a pan
4. Serve when ready

GAZPACHO SALAD

Serves: **4**

Prep Time: **10** Minutes

Cook Time: **30** Minutes

Total Time: **40** Minutes

INGREDIENTS

- ½ lb. cherry tomatoes
- ½ cucumber
- 3 oz. cooked quinoa
- 1 tsp bouillon powder
- 2 spring onions
- 1 red pepper
- ½ avocado
- 1 pack Japanese tofu

DIRECTIONS

1. **In a bowl combine all ingredients together**
2. **Add salad dressing, toss well and serve**

RADISH & PARSLEY SALAD

Serves: **4**

Prep Time: **10** Minutes

Cook Time: **30** Minutes

Total Time: **40** Minutes

INGREDIENTS

- 1 tsp olive oil
- ¼ lb. tomatoes
- 2 oz. radish
- 1 oz. parsley
- 1 tablespoon coriander
- salt

DIRECTIONS

1. In a bowl combine all ingredients together
2. Add salad dressing, toss well and serve

ZUCCHINI & BELL PEPPER SALAD

Serves: *1*

Prep Time: *5* Minutes

Cook Time: *5* Minutes

Total Time: *10* Minutes

INGREDIENTS

- ¼ cup zucchini
- ¼ cup red capsicum
- ½ cup yellow capsicum
- 1 cup sprouted moong
- ¼ cup apple
- 1 tablespoon olive oil
- 1 tsp lemon juice

DIRECTIONS

1. In a bowl combine all ingredients together
2. Add olive oil, toss well and serve

QUINOA & AVOCADO SALAD

Serves: *1*

Prep Time: 5 Minutes

Cook Time: 5 Minutes

Total Time: 10 Minutes

INGREDIENTS

- ¼ cooked quinoa
- ¼ cup avocado
- ¼ cup zucchini
- ¼ cup capsicum cubes
- ¼ cup mushroom
- ½ cup cherry tomatoes
- 1 cup lettuce
- 1 tablespoon sprouts
- 1 tsp olive oil
- Salad dressing

DIRECTIONS

1. In a bowl combine all ingredients together
2. Add salad dressing, toss well and serve

TOFU SALAD

Serves: **1**

Prep Time: **5** Minutes

Cook Time: **5** Minutes

Total Time: **10** Minutes

INGREDIENTS

- 1 pack tofu
- 1 cup chopped vegetables (carrots, cucumber)

DRESSING

- 1 tablespoon sesame oil
- 1 tablespoon mustard
- 1 tablespoon brown rice vinegar
- 1 tablespoon soya sauce

DIRECTIONS

1. **In a bowl combine all ingredients together**
2. **Add salad dressing, toss well and serve**

MIXED GREENS SALAD

Serves: **1**

Prep Time: **5** Minutes

Cook Time: **5** Minutes

Total Time: **10** Minutes

INGREDIENTS

- 2 cucumbers
- 3 radishes
- ¼ red bell pepper
- 2 spring onions
- 1 tablespoon red wine vinegar
- 1 tablespoon rice vinegar
- 1 tablespoon soya sauce
- 1 tablespoon clearspring mirin
- 2 cups mixed salad greens

DIRECTIONS

1. **In a bowl combine all ingredients together**
2. **Add salad dressing, toss well and serve**

QUINOA SALAD

Serves: **1**

Prep Time: **5** Minutes

Cook Time: **5** Minutes

Total Time: **10** Minutes

INGREDIENTS

- 1 cup cooked quinoa
- ¼ cup clearspring hijiki
- ¼ red bell pepper
- 1 bun watercress
- 2 radishes
- 2 tablespoons goji berries

DIRECTIONS

1. **In a bowl combine all ingredients together**
2. **Add salad dressing, toss well and serve**

ASPARAGUS FRITATTA

Serves: **2**

Prep Time: **10** Minutes

Cook Time: **20** Minutes

Total Time: **30** Minutes

INGREDIENTS

- ½ lb. asparagus
- 1 tablespoon olive oil
- ½ red onion
- ¼ tsp salt
- 1 cup egg substitute (egg allergy friendly)
- 2 oz. cheddar cheese
- 1 garlic clove
- ¼ tsp dill

DIRECTIONS

1. Boil the asparagus until tender and set aside
2. In a bowl whisk egg substitute with salt and cheese
3. In a frying pan heat olive oil and pour egg mixture
4. Add remaining ingredients and mix well
5. When ready serve with asparagus

BEETS FRITATTA

Serves: 2

Prep Time: 10 Minutes

Cook Time: 20 Minutes

Total Time: 30 Minutes

INGREDIENTS

- ½ lb. beets
- 1 tablespoon olive oil
- ½ red onion
- 1 cup egg substitute (egg allergy friendly)
- ¼ tsp salt
- 2 oz. cheddar cheese
- 1 garlic clove
- ¼ tsp dill

DIRECTIONS

1. In a bowl whisk egg substitute with salt and cheese
2. In a frying pan heat olive oil and pour egg mixture
3. Add remaining ingredients and mix well
4. Serve when ready

ARTICHOKE FRITATTA

Serves: 2

Prep Time: 10 Minutes

Cook Time: 20 Minutes

Total Time: 30 Minutes

INGREDIENTS

- 1 cup artichoke
- 1 tablespoon olive oil
- ½ red onion
- 1 cup egg substitute (egg allergy friendly)
- ¼ tsp salt
- 2 oz. cheddar cheese
- 1 garlic clove
- ¼ tsp dill

DIRECTIONS

1. In a bowl whisk egg substitute with salt and cheese
2. In a frying pan heat olive oil and pour egg mixture
3. Add remaining ingredients and mix well
4. Serve when ready

HAM FRITATTA

Serves: **2**

Prep Time: **10** Minutes

Cook Time: **20** Minutes

Total Time: **30** Minutes

INGREDIENTS

- 8-10 slices ham
- 1 tablespoon olive oil
- ½ red onion
- ¼ tsp salt
- 1 cup egg substitute (egg allergy friendly)
- 2 oz. parmesan cheese
- 1 garlic clove
- ¼ tsp dill

DIRECTIONS

1. In a bowl whisk eggs substitute with salt and parmesan cheese
2. In a frying pan heat olive oil and pour egg mixture
3. Add remaining ingredients and mix well
4. Serve when ready

BROCCOLI FRITATTA

Serves: 2

Prep Time: 10 Minutes

Cook Time: 20 Minutes

Total Time: 30 Minutes

INGREDIENTS

- 1 cup broccoli
- 1 tablespoon olive oil
- ½ red onion
- ¼ tsp salt
- 2 oz. cheddar cheese
- 1 garlic clove
- 1 cup egg substitute (egg allergy friendly)
- ¼ tsp dill

DIRECTIONS

1. In a skillet sauté broccoli until tender
2. In a bowl whisk egg substitute with salt and cheese
3. In a frying pan heat olive oil and pour egg mixture
4. Add remaining ingredients and mix well
5. When ready serve with sautéed broccoli

ROASTED SQUASH

Serves: **3-4**

Prep Time: **10** Minutes

Cook Time: **20** Minutes

Total Time: **30** Minutes

INGREDIENTS

- 2 delicata squashes
- 2 tablespoons olive oil
- 1 tsp curry powder
- 1 tsp salt

DIRECTIONS

1. Preheat the oven to 400 F
2. Cut everything in half lengthwise
3. Toss everything with olive oil and place onto a prepared baking sheet
4. Roast for 18-20 minutes at 400 F or until golden brown
5. When ready remove from the oven and serve

PIZZA

ZUCCHINI PIZZA

Serves: **6-8**

Prep Time: **10** Minutes

Cook Time: **15** Minutes

Total Time: **25** Minutes

INGREDIENTS

- 1 pizza crust
- ½ cup tomato sauce
- ¼ black pepper
- 1 cup zucchini slices
- 1 cup mozzarella cheese
- 1 cup olives

DIRECTIONS

1. Spread tomato sauce on the pizza crust
2. Place all the toppings on the pizza crust
3. Bake the pizza at 425 F for 12-15 minutes
4. When ready remove pizza from the oven and serve

SIMPLE PIZZA RECIPE

Serves: **6-8**
Prep Time: **10** Minutes
Cook Time: **15** Minutes
Total Time: **25** Minutes

INGREDIENTS

- 1 pizza crust gluten free
- ½ cup tomato sauce
- ¼ black pepper
- 1 cup pepperoni slices
- 1 cup mozzarella cheese
- 1 cup olives

DIRECTIONS

1. Spread tomato sauce on the pizza crust
2. Place all the toppings on the pizza crust
3. Bake the pizza at 425 F for 12-15 minutes
4. When ready remove pizza from the oven and serve

MUSHROOM PIZZA

Serves: **4**

Prep Time: **10** Minutes

Cook Time: **30** Minutes

Total Time: **40** Minutes

INGREDIENTS

- 3 mushrooms
- 3 oz. tomato paste
- 2 tablespoons avocado oil
- ¼ salt
- ¼ tsp dried basil
- 1 clove garlic

DIRECTIONS

1. **Preheat oven to 375 F**
2. **In a skillet add chopped mushrooms, garlic, basil and sauté for 2-3 minutes, transfer to a bowl**
3. **Add tomato paste and stir well**
4. **Fill each cavity of mushrooms with tomato paste and place into baking pan**
5. **Top with meat, cheese, olives and bake for 20-25 minutes**

THANK YOU FOR READING THIS BOOK!

CPSIA information can be obtained
at www.ICGtesting.com
Printed in the USA
BVHW071032040321
601713BV00007B/826